C000302564

A PORTRAIT OF
BRADFORD

A PORTRAIT OF
BRADFORD

JOHN MORRISON

HALSGROVE

First published in Great Britain in 2005

Copyright © 2005 text and photographs John Morrison

Title page: Bradford's coat of arms appears on top of the Ivegate Arch.

British Library Cataloguing-in-Publication Data
A CIP record for this title is available from the British Library

ISBN 1 84114 470 3

HALSGROVE
Halsgrove House
Lower Moor Way
Tiverton, Devon EX16 6SS
T: 01884 243242
F: 01884 243325
email: sales@halsgrove.com
website: www.halsgrove.com

Printed and bound by D'Auria Industrie Grafiche Spa, Italy

Introduction

When the borough of Bradford set up a tourism unit twenty-five years ago it, it made the jokey '...and finally' item on *News at Ten*. Bradford was a byword for industrial decline. The idea that people might want to spend time and money in Bradford, smoky old Bradford, well, it was a joke, wasn't it?

The city's success, built on textiles, seemed to belong to a very distant past. Visitors with a morbid taste for urban decay might have found something to interest them. But for other visitors, with a few days to spare and less specialised interests, what did Bradford have to offer?

When people stopped laughing and actually started to visit the borough of Bradford, they were pleasantly surprised. They found Haworth: a literary mecca to rival Stratford-upon-Avon. Here, in a small South Pennine town, the three Brontë sisters honed their precocious literary skills to produce books such as *Wuthering Heights* and *The Tenant of Wildfell Hall*.

They found Saltaire, the village built by Sir Titus Salt to house the workers at his mill – for many years the largest industrial building in the world. Remarkably, Saltaire has now joined the Taj Mahal and the Pyramids of Egypt as a World Heritage Site.

Visitors found Ilkley: a genteel spa town – almost an inland resort – where well-heeled hypochondriacs could socialise and take the Cold Water Cure. The town is overlooked by Ilkley Moor, criss-crossed by ancient tracks and marked with standing stones and rock carvings. A traverse of Ilkley Moor, with ham and eggs at Dick Hudson's pub, was a traditional day out for the millhands of Bradford. It was one such trip, to enjoy some bracing country air, that inspired the lyrics to *On Ilkley Moor 'Baht 'At*, which, despite dwelling morbidly on the inevitability of death, has become the unofficial anthem of Yorkshire.

The city of Bradford itself contains a wealth of buildings which recall the days when consignments of wool arrived daily from around the world to be combed, spun and woven in the mills. The Wool Exchange, City Hall, Lister's Mill and the warehouses of Little Germany were built on a monumental scale.

In terms of urban regeneration, Bradford has had a few false starts. Buildings of character fell to the wrecking ball during the 1960s and 1970s to make way for bland façades of concrete and glass. It's a tacit admission of failure by the town planners of the time that these buildings are now being demolished in their turn. There is a new 'regeneration masterplan' – full of grandiose, futuristic ideas for the centre of Bradford, including a lake. And why not? 'Bradford' is, after all, 'Broad Ford'; in five years we may be able to water-ski around the 'island' of City Hall. Since planners usually settle for the safe and sanitized option, I bet it won't happen. But wouldn't it be great?

Bradford's a proper place: not built just to be admired. No one who knows the city would ever call it pretty or picturesque. But has Stratford-upon-Avon got any World Heritage Sites? No, I didn't think so. You know, Bradford's tourism unit may well have the last laugh after all...

John Morrison
john@trunorth.demon.co.uk

Haworth Moor is not much changed since Charlotte Brontë found the
freedom and inspiration here to write *Wuthering Heights* in 1847.

A pair of sheep pose obligingly for the camera on the wild expanse of Keighley Moor.

An unconscious drama is played out against a backdrop of Bradford's Alhambra Theatre.

The façade of Bradford's City Hall in the early morning light.

A local's pub in Keighley, of a kind that's rapidly disappearing.

The workers at Salt's Mill lived in neat terraced houses –
the size of house depending on their status in the mill.

One of the statues which flank the
entrance to the Wool Exchange: Bishop
Blaise, the patron saint of woolcombers.

Grandad's Clock and Chair in
Chapel Street, Little Germany: my
favourite piece of sculpture in the city.

One flank of Sir Titus Salt's huge
mill at Saltaire, reflected above the weir
on the River Aire.

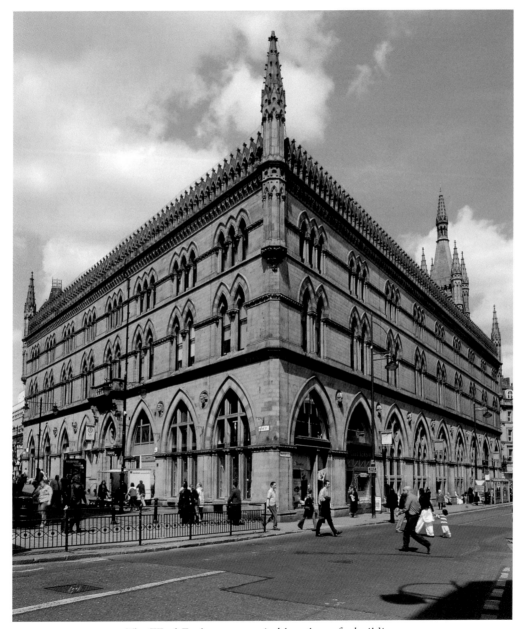

The Wool Exchange: a veritable palace of a building
that even the Medici family might have envied.

A narrowboat cruising the Leeds-Liverpool Canal, near Silsden.

An abstraction of cobbles, paving stones and saris, outside the Oastler Shopping Centre.

A proper ironmonger's shop in Queensbury: just the place to buy
nails by the pound or find a new handle for a yard-broom.

Bowing to popular demand, the Commercial pub in Esholt was renamed
The Woolpack, after it featured in the long-running soap, *Emmerdale*.

The towns infiltrate into the countryside round these parts, and slivers of green penetrate the towns. This is near Oakworth.

Typical scenery near Stanbury, to the north of Bradford: isolated farms, drystone walls and fields laid in green velour.

Multicultural percussion during a Family Day in Lister Park: part of the Bradford Festival.

Musicianship, good humour and death-defying stunts: what
more could you want on a sunny afternoon in the park?

A woman is caught in a shaft of sunlight and framed by the doorway of the Wool Exchange.

As part of the city's regeneration, some buildings are being wiped off the map; others are being restored.

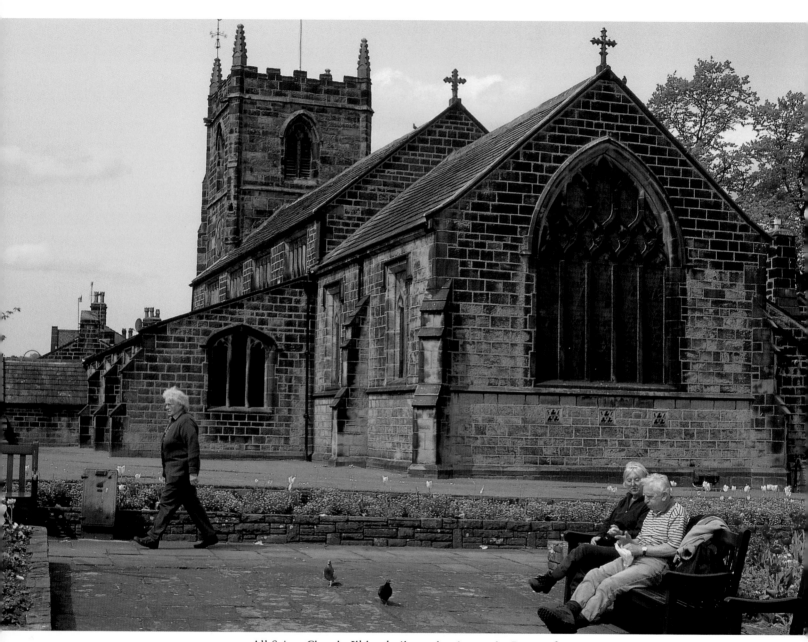

All Saints Church, Ilkley, built on the site on the Roman fort
of *Olicana*; look inside to find three Saxon crosses.

Sir Titus Salt incorporated this decorative row of almshouses into the plan of his 'model village'.

A group of cottages behind a weir on Silsden Beck.

The people of Bingley waited many years for this ring road to be built;
bizarrely it has even won an architectural award.

The Mela is Bradford's annual celebration of Asian culture.
'Take our picture', said this group of girls... so I did.

The Bradford Festival brings colour, light and music to Centenary Square.

Undercliffe Cemetery comes second in splendour only to London's Highgate. This is where many prominent Bradford mill-owners and their families were laid to rest.

There are many reservoirs dotted around Bradford, built to slake the thirst of nearby milltowns. Doe Park Reservoir, near Denholme, has a thriving sailing club.

Salt's Mill creates a stone canyon on both sides of the Leeds-Liverpool Canal.

Hall Ings: a street that will look very different once the city's regeneration is complete.

The Botanical Gardens in Lister Park, named after Samuel
Cunliffe Lister, who made his fortune in the woollen trade.

Paths criss-cross through the bluebells in Middleton Woods, near Ilkley.

The bold symmetry of Cartwright Hall...

...one of the city's architectural gems.

Five Rise Locks, on the Leeds-Liverpool Canal near Bingley,
were constructed to overcome a sixty-foot gradient.

The view of Bingley – and the famous Damart thermal underwear factory –
from the top of Five Rise Locks on the Leeds-Liverpool Canal.

A statue of Samuel Cunliffe Lister, in a corner of the park that bears his name.

Even when the millhands were relaxing in Roberts Park, near Saltaire, they would still be under the watchful gaze of their autocratic employer, Sir Titus Salt.

A lonely farmhouse near Keighley, lit up by
a ray of sunlight out of a stormy sky.

Newsholme Dean, a delightful wooded valley near Keighley: a secret only known to locals.

Foster Square will be a building site — and a hard-hat area —
until the new Broadway Shopping Centre is completed.

If the portrait on the left is meant to be of Joe Johnson, Bradford-born
world snooker champion of 1986, then Joe should sue for defamation.

Jacobs Well: nice pub... shame about the building behind,
an ugly monstrosity that shares its name.

The Friendly Inn, Keighley, whose sign features two hands clasped in conviviality.

Storm clouds mass over Bradford, seen from the vantage point of
Queensbury, leaving Lister's Mill lit up by a shaft of sunlight.

A Land Rover tackles the old road between Haworth and
Hebden Bridge as it rises to the top of Cock Hill.

An interplay of shadows in the heart of the city.

A piece of modern sculpture that actually *works*: 'Fibres', by Ian Randall, sited near Foster Square railway station.

Bradford's Mela is a two-day celebration of Asian culture, music and food.

The lion lays down with the lamb at the Mela, as does
Pooh Bear with one of the 101 Dalmations.

The Old Manor House, Ilkley: a handsome house, built on the site
of the Roman fort, now a museum and art gallery.

Now marooned in the suburbs of Bradford, Bolling Hall is a seventeenth
century manor house that incorporates a medieval pele tower.

The sidings at Haworth, one of the five stations on the Keighley & Worth Valley Railway.

If Oakworth Station looks strangely familiar, that's because it
starred in the much-loved film, *The Railway Children*.

The campus of Bradford University, granted its charter as recently as 1966.

A surreal example of the signwriter's art, on Allerton Road in Bradford.

The boating lake in Lister Park is a popular place to
while away a sunny Sunday; hire a boat...

… or bring a bike.

A match at Denholme Cricket Club, shot from inside the tiny scorebox.

An aquaduct near Bingley, where the Leeds-Liverpool
Canal is carried across the River Aire.

Now just another suburb of Bradford, the old village of Thornton has a ramshackle charm.

A quiet corner of Haworth (and, with the number of visitors, there aren't too many of those).

White Wells, overlooking Ilkley, was the town's orginal spa,
where people flocked to 'take the waters'.

The 'calf' of the Cow and Calf rocks, near Ilkley. There used to be a bull,
to complete the family unit, until it was broken up for building stone.

The Twelve Apostles: one of the many relics of early man that can be found on Ilkley Moor.

A milestone which would have helped to guide weary travellers across Ilkley Moor.

The Cow and Calf rocks, overlooking lower Wharfedale, is one of the most famous landmarks in Yorkshire...

...where climbers can practise their
holds and belays.

Evening sunlight emphasises the texture of a rockface at the Cow and Calf.

Snowy fields around Thornton, lit by pale winter sunshine.

A characterful cottage in Low Green, Bradford, known as the Doll's House.

Shopping spills out onto the streets in a suburb of Bradford.

East Riddlesden Hall, near Keighley: a splendid example
of a 'Halifax House', with a rose window at the
rear to match the one at the front.

Blossom in Haworth Park: the candyfloss colours of spring.

A moment of quiet reflection on the
splendidly-named Hustlergate.

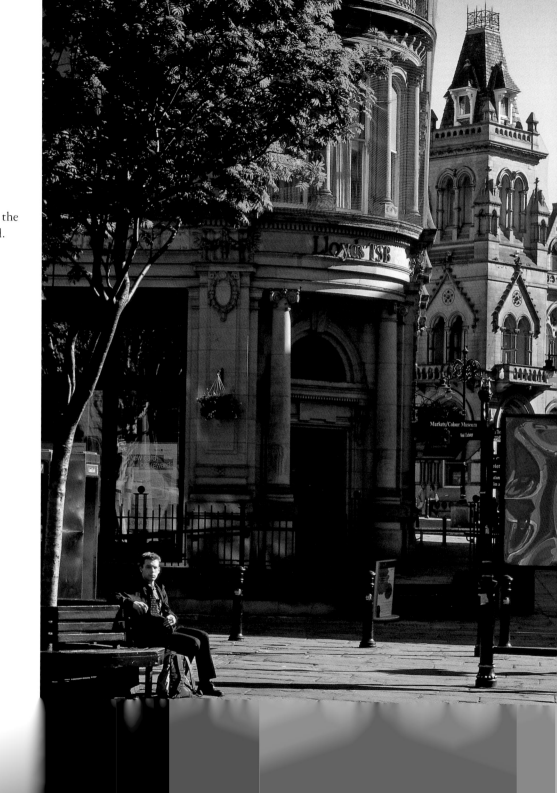

A corner of New Market Place, with the Wool Exchange in the background.

Cliffe Castle, in Keighley: a castle in name only,
actually built as a lavish home by by a wealthy worsted
manufacturer, and now the town's museum.

Cricket in Roberts Park, Saltaire, with the chimney of Salt's Mill in the background.

The unassuming terrace house on Market Street in
Thornton, where the Brontë sisters were born.

Mist on a damp autumn day makes
the graveyard at Haworth look
particularly atmospheric.

Early morning reveals the stillness and sculptural qualities of the Mughal Water Gardens in Lister Park…

…while later in the day they become a playground.

One day, if the planners hold their nerve, City Park could be submerged beneath the water of City Lake.

Office workers gather in Centenary Square during their lunch hour.

An old milestone...

... beside the ruler-straight Roman road that onced linked *Olicana* with the forts across the Pennines.

A roofscape in Bradford city centre – including the domes of
the Alhambra Theatre and the old Odeon cinema.

Originally built as the Sion Jubilee Baptist Church in Little
Germany, this handsome building is now a Sikh temple.

The arch of a bridge on the Leeds-Liverpool Canal,
near Bingley, creates a pleasing symmetry.

A quiet moment with a book at Appley Bridge, where
the Leeds-Liverpool Canal broadens out into a marina.

Victoria Hall, Saltaire, where the millhands could enjoy musical performances.

Cyclists on the towpath of the Leeds-Liverpool Canal are dwarfed by the bulk of Salt's New Mill.

Muck and brass in proverbial conjunction at Keighley
(with the Yorkshire Dales in the distance).

A scene in West Horton that can be replicated all around Bradford:
terraced houses cheek-by-jowl with industry.

The colours of spring…

...and autumn – come to Judy Woods, near Wyke.

Sunlight picks out the monumental façade of Salt's Mill…

... dwarfing the terraced houses.

The towpath of the Leeds-Liverpool Canal, near Appley Bridge.

Fish and chips outdoors, on a sunny spring day in
Addingham, where West Yorkshire meets the Dales.

Bradford's Alhambra Theatre is one of the city's big success stories...

... no wonder it's lit up at night.

A statue of J B Priestley, the man who brought Bradford to the world
– barely disguised in his writing as smoky 'Bruddersford'.

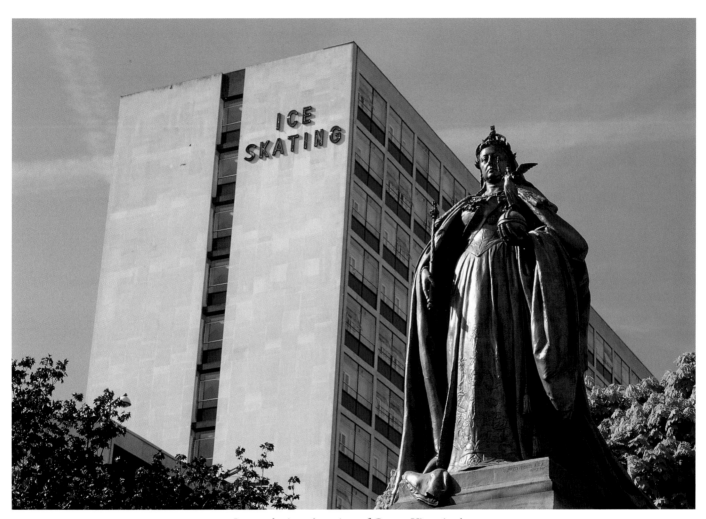

It was during the reign of Queen Victoria that
Bradford's fortunes changed most dramatically.

A steam train on the restored Keighley and Worth Valley Railway, pulling into Oakworth Station.

One of those perfect spring days, when the landscape is as colourful as it will be all year; this is Addingham Church.

Silsden: waiting for Jeff the Barber to open up.

Betty's Tearoom, on the Grove in Ilkley, is *the* place to relax after giving
the credit cards some hammer in the town's smart shops.

One of the most recent additions to the city's public artworks is this sculpture on Duke Street, entitled 'Connecting the City'.

A statue of Richard Oastler, who campaigned tirelessly for better wages and shorter hours for the children who laboured in the mills.

Traditional stone cottages, with heavy stone door lintels
and window frames, in Cross Road, near Keighley...

...and the village of Harden.

The pedestrian concourse and Market Place in Shipley.

A little fountain in City Park called 'Bradford-by-the-Sea', against the façade of City Hall.

It's a sign of how many Japanese tourists visit Haworth that directions
to places with Brontë connections are in Japanese as well as English.

An unfortunate juxtaposition of signs on the approach into Bradford.

'Homage to Delius', a piece of sculpture honouring the Bradford-born
composer (the feeling wasn't mutual – 'I hate the place', he wrote).

Kirkgate, one of Bradford's busiest shopping streets, with the Kirkgate Centre at the top.

Spring comes to Stanbury, with a procession of new-born lambs.

A view familiar to those who drive 'over the tops' from Keighley to Hebden Bridge:
Haworth Moor, Leeshaw Reservoir and fields of buttercups.

The first warm weekend of spring encourages families to head
for the River Wharfe at Ilkley, and its own strip of beach.

The Shipley Glen Tramway has been carrying people up to the glen,
Baildon Moor and beyond for more than a century.

Architectural details, in Little Germany…

... and Bradford city centre.

The cobbled street of Haworth looking particularly moody in a clinging mist.

A peaceful tête-a-tête against a
backdrop of concrete and glass.

Allotments near Bingley: a quiet corner going back to nature.

One more reason to shop at Morrisons, the Bradford-based
supermarket group: the bags will keep the birds away.

Centenary Square: on sunny days it's a place for lovers and loners, lechers and loafers.

Paper Hall, the oldest secular building in Bradford, dates from 1643.
The first Spinny Jenny in the city was set up here, helping to
mechanise the textile industries.

The Parsonage at Haworth, overlooking the graveyard, was home
to the Brontë sisters for most of their tragically-short lives.

The façade of City Hall and the bridge which carries pedestrians across Hall Ings.

A cobbled street in Saltaire, punctuated by
one of the chimneys of Salt's Mill.

The warehouse district of Little Germany – a name which reflects the number of German merchants in the city's woollen trade.

The Wool Exchange now houses a coffee house and bookshop.

Trees weighed down with blossom, surrounding Keighley's Town Hall Square.

Colour and costumes in Lister Park…

...during the Bradford Festival.

A century and a half after it was built, Salt's Mill still dominates its
surroundings – especially when picked out by autumn sunlight.